flavoring with
Spices

flavoring with
Spices

Clare Gordon-Smith

photography by

James Merrell

RYLAND
PETERS
& SMALL

LONDON NEW YORK

Art Director **Jacqui Small**
Art Editor **Penny Stock**
Design Assistant **Mark Latter**
Editor **Elsa Petersen-Schepelern**
Photography **James Merrell**
Food Stylist **Lucy McKelvie**
Stylist **Sue Skeen**
Production Consultant **Vincent Smith**

**Our thanks to Christine Walsh and Ian Bartlett, and
Sally Everett of Food Link (Eastern) Ltd.**

First published in the USA in 1996
First published by Ryland Peters & Small, Inc. in 2000
519 Broadway, 5th Floor
New York, NY 10012
www.rylandpeters.com

This paperback edition first published in 2003
10 9 8 7 6 5 4 3 2 1

Text copyright © Clare Gordon-Smith 1996
Design and photographs copyright © Ryland Peters & Small 1996

Library of Congress Cataloging-in-Publication Data

Gordon-Smith, Clare.
 [Basic flavorings. Spices.]
 Flavoring with spices / Clare Gordon-Smith ; photography by James
Merrell.
     p. cm.
Originally published under title: Basic flavorings. Spices. Philadelphia
: Courage Books, 1996.
Includes index.
 ISBN 1-84172-447-5
1. Cookery (Spices) I. Title.
 TX819.A1 G67 2003
 641.6'383–dc21

                    2002013434

Printed and bound in China.

Notes:
Ovens should be preheated to the
specified temperature. If using a
convection oven, adjust time and
temperature according to the
manufacturer's instructions.

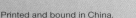

Spices are the bark, seeds, roots, or pods of various aromatic plants. Once, spices like ginger and tamarind were always dried, but thanks to modern transport, some can now be found fresh.

Spice mixtures are used in all the world's great cuisines, and many use blends peculiar to their own areas, and to particular dishes. Best freshly ground, they can also be bought prepared. Shown here before grinding are some of the most famous blends. Back row, from left: India's classic spice mixture, **garam masala** (recipe page 36), including cloves, pepper, cumin, cinnamon, nutmeg, and mace, varies from area to area; Morocco's **ras-el-hanout**, a mix of spices, rosebuds and lavender; and the Jamaican **jerk seasoning**, moistened with garlic and lime juice, used to spice meat dishes. Front row, from left are the ingredients for **curry powder** (recipe page 16); classic **pickling spice** with mustard seeds, peppercorns, mace, chiles, allspice, and dill seed; and traditional American **mixed spice**, with nutmeg, cinnamon, ginger, and cloves, used in pies and cakes.

the flavors of
Spices

Cassia bark | Paprika | Nutmeg | Mace | Vanilla beans | Caraway seeds

Mustard seeds | Ginger | Star anise | Saffron

A selection of spices—fresh, dried, flaked, or ground. **Cassia bark** is sometimes used instead of cinnamon. Powdered **paprika** from Hungary ranges in taste from mild to hot. Black **mustard seeds** are used in India and Nepal as well as in prepared mustards. Whole **nutmeg** are best freshly grated, but ground nutmeg is widely available. Russet-colored **mace**, the lacy covering of the nutmeg, can be bought whole or ground, and is more subtle than nutmeg. **Ginger,** like **horseradish** and **galangal,** is a hot, pungent root, available fresh, dried, and flaked (shown). **Vanilla beans** can be used again and again, and kept in a jar of sugar (which can be used to flavor puddings and desserts

8 The flavors of spices

Cinnamon sticks

Turmeric powder

Turmeric roots

Tamarind pods

Black cardamom pods

Green cardamom pods

Juniper berries

Cloves

White peppercorns

Allspice

araway seeds flavor bread and cakes in
rthern Europe. Star-shaped **star anise**
s an aniseed taste. Expensive **saffron**
ands are the dried stigmas of the saffron
cus plant. **Cinnamon** sticks are also
ilable in ground form. Yellow **turmeric**
made from a ginger-like root. **Cloves** are
 of the world's most popular spices.

Jamaican **allspice** has a
mixed-spice flavor. Velvety **tamarind** pods
contain lemony pulp and seeds. **White
peppercorns** are black pepper with the
outer shell removed. Large black and smaller
green **cardamom** pods contain lots of tiny,
aromatic black seeds. Large, black, shiny
juniper berries are the main flavor in gin.

Appetizers

Sautéed shrimp
with turmeric and mustard seeds

India is the home of many of the world's most wonderful spices, so Indian cooks are masters at using them in all kinds of cooking. Seaside holiday resorts in India, such as Goa and Kerala, are great places to eat fresh seafood spiced in the most delicious and unusual ways.

Peel the shrimp, but leave the little tail fins intact. Place the shrimp in a bowl. Mix the turmeric and chili powder together, sprinkle over the shrimp, toss well, and lightly rub the mixture into the flesh. Heat the oil in a large skillet and, when very hot, add the mustard seeds. When the seeds start popping, add the crushed garlic and sauté until golden, then stir in the chopped green chile. Add the shrimp and sauté over a high heat for about 2 to 3 minutes until they become opaque. Remove immediately to a serving plate—do not overcook. Sprinkle with salt and the chopped fresh cilantro leaves, then serve with crispy poppadoms, if available.

12 medium-size raw shrimp

pinch of turmeric

pinch of chili powder

4 tablespoons sunflower oil

½ teaspoon black mustard seeds

4 garlic cloves, crushed

1 fresh hot green chile, finely chopped

1 tablespoon torn fresh cilantro leaves

coarse sea salt

crispy poppadoms, to serve (optional)

Serves 4

Hot tortillas
filled with spiced crab

Crab forms a great partnership with ginger
or chiles in many cuisines around the world.
This one is based on a Mexican original,
teamed with a zippy avocado salsa.

To prepare the salsa, place the avocado in a bowl,
and toss in the lemon juice. Stir in the remaining
ingredients, and set aside to develop the flavors
while you prepare the filling.
To prepare the filling, heat the olive oil in a non-stick
skillet, add the onion, garlic, and ginger, and cook
for 2 to 3 minutes, until golden. Stir in the coriander,
cumin, crabmeat, tomatoes, salt, and pepper.
Heat the tortillas in a dry skillet, then place the filling
over half of each one. Wrap the other half over the
top of the filling, and serve with the avocado salsa.

1 tablespoon olive oil

1 onion, finely chopped

2 garlic cloves, crushed

1-inch piece of
fresh ginger, minced

1 teaspoon coriander
seeds or powder

½ teaspoon cumin

8 oz. fresh crabmeat

2 plum tomatoes
peeled, seeded
and chopped

salt and pepper

1 packet flour tortillas

avocado salsa

1 avocado, sliced

2 teaspoons lemon juice

1 red onion, sliced

2 tablespoons chopped
fresh cilantro leaves

juice and grated zest
of 1 lime

pinch of cayenne

s

Serves

coriander and cumin are great

with crab—in an extra **spicy partnership**

Caribbean chicken
with ginger and star anise

4 chicken breasts

1 oz. fresh ginger

3 star anise

3 tablespoons sherry

⅔ cup stock

3 garlic cloves, crushed

2 bay leaves

⅔ cup olive oil

⅔ cup white wine vinegar

2 white onions, sliced

salt and 8 peppercorns

Use chicken or vegetable stock for this recipe, and then add sprigs of basil or rosemary for more herb flavor.

Bone the chicken breasts, crush the ginger and star anise, and place in a saucepan with the chicken, sherry, and stock. Simmer for 20 minutes until the chicken is tender. Slice the chicken into thin strips and place in a bowl with the crushed garlic, bay leaves, olive oil, vinegar, onions, salt, and pepper. Mix well and leave to marinate in the refrigerator for about 2 days before serving. Serve with a spinach salad and lemon wedges.

Eggplant dip
with coriander and sesame seeds

4 eggplants, halved

2 tablespoons chile oil

1 oz. coriander seeds

1 oz. sesame seeds

4–6 garlic cloves

1 oz. fresh ginger

1 oz. coconut cream

salt

Brush the eggplant with chile oil. Cook in a preheated oven at 400°F for 40 minutes until soft, then scrape the flesh into a bowl. Crush the coriander seeds, then dry fry them with the sesame seeds for 1 minute to release the flavors. Crush the garlic and ginger. Gently heat the coconut cream in a saucepan. Mix all the ingredients together to form a paste. Place in a serving bowl and serve either warm or chilled, with pita breads.

Serves 4

Curried parsnip soup
with crème fraîche

A very English recipe—using curry powder, a spice mixture that originated in England. Though the British brought it back from India, it is a mixture that no Indian cook would recognize. It goes particularly well with sweet young parsnips. Homemade curry powder is vastly superior to the store-bought kind. Mix 3 tablespoons coriander seeds with 1 teaspoon each of fenugreek, ground ginger, and peppercorns, 2 tablespoons each of cumin seeds, mustard seeds, and turmeric, plus a cinnamon stick, and 3 dried chiles. Place in a spice or coffee grinder, grind to a fine powder, keep in an airtight jar and use as quickly as possible.

Melt the butter very gently in a saucepan, stir in the curry powder, and cook for 1 minute. Add the parsnips, salt, pepper, and vegetable stock, bring to a boil, and simmer for about 20 minutes. Pour into a blender or food processor and puree until smooth. Add extra stock if you prefer a thinner soup. Reheat and serve with a dollop of crème fraîche, a sprinkling of paprika or curry powder, and crusty wholegrain bread.

2 tablespoons butter

1 tablespoon curry
powder, store-bought
or homemade (see
recipe introduction
opposite)

1 lb. young parsnips,
roughly chopped

2½ cups
vegetable stock

salt and freshly
ground black pepper

to serve

⅔ cup crème fraîche,

paprika or curry powder

Serves 4

a classic soup **partnership**—parsnips

with curry powder to give extra zip

Jamaican pumpkin soup
with spiced cream

Cooks in Jamaica and the other Caribbean islands really know their spices! This recipe uses chiles and ground ginger in the soup, and lots of spices in the cream garnish. Use chopped jalapeños for extra heat or, for an unusual, spicy, fruity flavor, a whole Scotch bonnet chile, removed (unbroken) just before pureeing in the blender.

To make the spiced cream, place the crème fraîche in a bowl, stir in the spices, and set aside to infuse. To make the soup, peel the pumpkin, scrape out the seeds with a spoon, and cut the flesh into 1-inch pieces. Seed and dice the chiles. Place the butter in a large saucepan and melt over medium heat. Add the onion, carrot, and celery, and sauté until softened and transparent. Stir in the garlic and chiles, then cook for 1 minute. Add the pumpkin, chicken stock, herbs, ginger, and seasoning. Bring to a boil, reduce the heat, and simmer for 20 minutes until the vegetables are soft. Remove the bay leaves and thyme, pour into a blender or food processor, add the cream, then puree until smooth. Thin with stock if necessary. Serve with a large dollop of spiced cream on top.

1 lb. pumpkin

2 jalapeño chiles

2 tablespoons butter

1 onion, diced

1 carrot, diced

1 celery stalk, diced

3 garlic cloves, crushed

5 cups chicken stock

2 bay leaves

2 sprigs of thyme

4 tablespoons chopped fresh flat-leaf parsley

pinch of ground ginger

1¼ cups cream

salt and pepper

spiced cream

⅔ cup crème fraîche

pinch of ground cumin

pinch of coriander

pinch of cayenne

1 tablespoon snipped fresh chives

Serves

Entrees

Seared salmon
in spicy ginger marinade

They don't have salmon in Asia, but Asian spices marry wonderfully with this rich king of fishes—as demonstrated in this rather Pan-Pacific recipe. If you're serving large fennel bulbs with this dish, cut them into quarters, brush with oil, and bake in a hot oven until tender and crispy brown around the edges.

To make the marinade, mix all the ingredients together in a shallow bowl.
Add the salmon fillet and turn several times in order to coat with the marinade. Place in the refrigerator for at least 2 hours.
When ready to cook, remove the fish from the marinade and pat dry with paper towels. Dust the fish with the ground star anise. Heat a stove-top grill pan, add the fish, and sear on both sides.
Serve with roasted fennel.

1 large salmon fillet, about 1 lb.

pinch of ground star anise

roasted baby fennel, or fennel bulbs, to serve

spicy ginger marinade

2 tablespoons soy sauce

6 star anise, crushed

4 tablespoons vermouth

1-inch piece of fresh ginger, finely sliced

1 garlic clove, crushed

2 tablespoons chopped fresh cilantro

1 hot red chile, seeded and chopped

Serves 4

Steamed monkfish
with creamy coconut rice

Thai cooking is one of the most interesting spice-based cuisines. This recipe uses a mixture of spices spread over the fish before steaming, and a complementary mixture to perfume the delicious, sticky Thai-spiced rice, served in pretty banana leaf pillows. If you can't find banana leaves, substitute foil, or omit the final steaming of the rice.

To make the spiced rice, heat the oil in a skillet, add the onion, and sauté gently until golden. Add the cardamom seeds and seasoning, and cook for 1 minute more. Stir in the rice and coconut cream, followed by the water, and cook for about 10 minutes until just tender. Drain and wrap in banana leaves. To prepare the spice mixture, mince the ginger and mix with the remaining ingredients. Press the mixture on top of the monkfish fillets. Place the fish and the banana leaf pillows in a bamboo steamer set over a saucepan of simmering water. Steam for about 5 minutes until the flesh becomes opaque, then serve immediately, garnished with slices of fresh kaffir lime.

cardamom, cumin, and turmeric—

delicious with coconut Thai rice and fish

4 monkfish fillets

sliced kaffir limes, to serve

spice mixture

1 inch fresh ginger

pinch of ground coriander

pinch of ground cumin

pinch of turmeric

2 cloves

1 onion, finely chopped

2 hot green chiles

1 garlic clove, crushed

coconut rice

2 tablespoons corn o

1 small onion, diced

crushed seeds fro 3 cardamom po

2 cups Thai ri

½ cup coconut crea

scant 2 cups wa

banana lea

salt and pep

Serve

Roasted cod
with a spicy, crunchy crust

Horseradish is a spice that's usually eaten fresh, since it loses much of its pungency when heated. However, that isn't always a disadvantage, as this unusual recipe proves.

To make the tartar sauce, mix all the ingredients together and set aside to develop the flavor.

To make the horseradish crust, mix together the lemon rind, breadcrumbs, crushed coriander seeds, parsley, horseradish, salt, and pepper.

Place the cod steaks in a shallow roasting pan and season with salt and pepper.

Press the crust mixture firmly onto the steaks.

Bake in a preheated oven at 400°F for about 10 to 15 minutes until the flesh is white and milky.

To serve, place the roasted cod on 4 heated dinner plates and serve the tartar sauce separately.

Serve with saffron mashed potatoes and steamed baby leeks.

hot **horseradish** paired with cr

an East-meets

...nder seeds—

...e combination

4 cod steaks

salt and freshly
ground black pepper

spicy crust

grated rind of 1 lemon

½ cup breadcrumbs

1 tablespoon crushed
coriander seeds

2 tablespoons chopped
fresh flat-leaf parsley

2 oz. fresh horseradish,
minced

salt and freshly
ground black pepper

tartar sauce

6 medium dill pickles,
finely chopped

1 cup crème fraîche

2 tablespoons chopped
fresh flat-leaf parsley

1 teaspoon
caraway seeds

1 teaspoon
fennel seeds

salt and freshly
ground black pepper

Serves 4

Sesame roasted tuna
in orange and star anise marinade

Honey, oil, and soy sauce make wonderful marinades. The honey helps all the flavors stick to the food, and you can vary the kind of soy sauce—dark soy has more flavor, but darkens the food; light soy is more subtle.

Place the tuna fillet in a shallow dish, beat the marinade ingredients together, pour over the fish, and chill for a few hours.

Place the sweet potato chips in a roasting pan, and sprinkle with the olive oil and salt. Cook in a preheated oven at 400°F for 15 minutes.

Meanwhile, drain the tuna, pat dry on paper towels, then brush with sesame oil.

Add the tuna to the roasting pan and continue to cook for about 10 to 15 minutes, until the fish is tender but still pink in the middle, and the potatoes are golden brown, and soft when pierced with a fork.

Serve with a green salad.

1 lb. tuna fillet

2 sweet potatoes, peeled and sliced into fat, chunky chips

sea salt

olive oil, for roasting

sesame oil, for brushing

orange and star anise marinade

4 tablespoons soy sauce

grated rind and juice of 2 oranges

2 tablespoons honey

1 tablespoon sesame oil

2 garlic cloves, crushed

1-inch piece of fresh ginger, minced

2 strips lemon zest

1 star anise

1 tablespoon sesame seeds, toasted

Serves 4

Seven-spice squid
with chile dipping sauce

The Japanese and Thai both make a seven-spice mixture. This recipe uses the Thai mix.

2 tablespoons rice vinegar

2 teaspoons mustard seeds

2 small chiles, sliced

1 egg white

2 tablespoons cream

16 small squid, cleaned

oil, for frying

seven-spice flour

1 cup plain flour

1½ teaspoons salt

3 tablespoons sesame seeds

2 teaspoons mustard seeds

1 teaspoon coriander seeds

1 teaspoon seven-spice powder

Serves 4

To make a chile and mustard seed dipping sauce, pour the rice vinegar into a small bowl, then add the mustard seeds and sliced chiles. Set aside to infuse while you prepare the squid.

To prepare the seven-spice flour, mix all the ingredients together, then spread on a plate.

To prepare the squid coating, beat the egg white and cream together, then dip the squid into the mixture. Press the squid firmly into the spiced flour mixture so the fish is well covered with spices on all sides.

To cook the squid, heat the oil in a skillet, add the coated fish, and sauté for about 3 minutes until golden brown.

Remove from the skillet and drain on paper towels. Serve immediately, with a bowl of the chile and mustard seed dipping sauce.

Tamarind lamb chops
with guava jelly

Tamarind is used a little like lemon juice—to give a sharp flavor. You can buy it in brown velvety pods, in blocks of paste (pictured below left) you have to reconstitute in boiling water, or as a ready made puree. It contrasts well with the rich sweetness of guava jelly, which you can buy in bottles in Caribbean or Asian markets—or even make your own using fresh or canned guava juice.

If using tamarind paste, crumble the paste, place it in a large saucepan, cover with water, bring to a boil, and simmer over a medium-low heat for about 30 minutes, until soft. Push through a sieve, and discard the seeds and strings.

To make the sauce, heat the oil over a low heat, add the shallots, salt, and pepper, and sauté until golden. Add the garlic, cook for 2 minutes, then add the stock and tamarind pulp or puree. Bring to a boil, and simmer for 10 minutes. Stir in the cayenne and honey. Remove from the heat and keep warm.

Brush the lamb chops with oil. Mix the pepper, sesame seeds, and cumin seeds in a shallow bowl, then press the chops onto the mixture until they are well coated with seeds. Set aside.

Heat the oil in a skillet and sauté the chops until the seeds are golden and the meat cooked to your liking. Serve with parsnip chips, the tamarind sauce, and guava jelly.

8 lamb chops

freshly ground black pepper

3 tablespoons sesame seeds

3 tablespoons cumin seeds

oil, for brushing and cooking

tamarind sauce

6 oz. tamarind paste, or 6 tablespoons tamarind puree

1 tablespoon olive oil

6 shallots, diced

2 garlic cloves, crushed

1¼ cups chicken or vegetable stock

pinch of cayenne

1½ tablespoons honey

salt and freshly ground black pepper

to serve

parsnip chips

guava jelly

Serves

Malaysian lamb curry
with green curry paste

A sweet, mild curry made with galangal, a cousin of ginger, which is usually available either fresh or powdered in Asian markets. This recipe uses powdered galangal, but 2 teaspoons of minced fresh galangal could be used instead. If you can't find it, half the quantity of ginger is a suitable substitute. Kaffir lime leaves can also be found in Asian markets, but if they're not available, you can substitute grated lime zest.

To make the green curry paste, peel the ginger and place in a blender with the chiles, garlic, and cilantro, and puree until smooth. Set aside until ready to use.
To make the curry, heat the oil in a deep skillet, add the shallot and cook until soft. Add the cubes of lamb and sauté until browned. Add the green curry paste, ground ginger, turmeric, coriander seeds, cinnamon, galangal, cumin seeds, lime leaves, and coconut cream and gently simmer for 40 minutes Slice the eggplant, add to the skillet and simmer for a further 20 minutes.
Serve with the crispy fried onions and Thai rice.

⅔ cup olive oil

1 shallot, chopped

2 lb. leg of lamb,
boned and cubed

2 teaspoons
ground ginger

1 teaspoon turmeric

2 teaspoons coriander
seeds, roasted

1 cinnamon stick

1 teaspoon galangal

½ teaspoon
cumin seeds

3 kaffir lime leaves

2½ cups coconut cream

2 small eggplants

crispy fried onions,
to serve

green curry
paste

2 oz. fresh ginger

5 whole green chiles

4 garlic cloves

leaves from 1 bunch
of fresh cilantro

Serves 4

Coconut chicken
with garlic and ginger sauce

Ginger is the spice used in this recipe. Once regarded as a spice only when dried, modern transport and farming methods mean that now we can have spices like this in their fresh form—a slightly different taste, but one which many people prefer.

2 tablespoons
sweet butter

1 tablespoon olive oil

8 chicken pieces

2 shallots, chopped

1 garlic clove, crushed

1-inch piece of
fresh ginger, minced

1 cup coconut milk

2 tablespoons orange
or kumquat marmalade

salt and black
freshly ground pepper

⅔ cup shredded
coconut, toasted,
to serve

Serves 4

Heat the butter and olive oil in a large skillet, add the chicken and cook for about 3 to 4 minutes until browned on all sides. Remove from the skillet with a slotted spoon and set aside in a warm place. Add the shallots, garlic, and ginger to the skillet and sauté for 2 minutes, until softened and transparent. Return the browned chicken to the skillet and stir in the coconut milk, marmalade and seasoning. Simmer, uncovered, for about 5 to 10 minutes, or until the chicken is tender. Sprinkle with the toasted coconut and serve with fragrant Thai rice.

Baked chicken breasts
with chiles and spiced cream

Indian cooks always grind their garam masalas (spice mixtures) freshly each day, sautéing them first, to release all the flavors from the wonderful volatile oils.
Every family has its own masala mix, but a typical blend might include 2 tablespoons each of coriander and cardamom seeds, 1 teaspoon each of cumin, peppercorns and cloves, 1 cinnamon stick, and ½ teaspoon each of ground nutmeg and mace.

To make the spiced cream, mix the tomato puree with the mustard, cumin, garam masala, lemon juice, salt, chilli powder and cream. Set aside.
To prepare the chicken, cut the breasts off the bone. Crush the cardamom pods, and slice the ginger and seeded chiles into fine strips. Heat 3 tablespoons of the oil in a skillet, and sauté the cloves, cinnamon, and cardamom for 1 minute. Add the chicken, brown on both sides, then transfer to an ovenproof pan.
Add the onion, ginger, and chiles to the skillet, stir-fry until lightly browned, then spread over the chicken. Heat the remaining oil in the skillet, add the mustard seeds, and sauté until they start to pop. Add the garlic and cook until golden. Add the spiced cream, heat to a simmer, pour over the chicken, season, and cook in a preheated oven at 350°F for 25 minutes, or until the chicken is tender.
Serve with cabbage stir-fried with garlic and chile.

4 chicken breasts

6 cardamom pods

1 oz. fresh ginger

3 hot green chiles

4 tablespoons corn oil

6 cloves

1 cinnamon stick

1 onion, sliced

½ teaspoon black or yellow mustard seeds

1 garlic clove, crushed

salt and pepper

spiced cream

2 tablespoon tomato puree

1 tablespoon Dijon mustard

pinch of ground cumin

pinch of garam masala

lemon juice, to taste

½ teaspoon salt

pinch of chili powder

1 cup heavy cream

Serve

Indian cooks **sauté their spices** to release

their **wonderful aromas** before adding them to the dish

Gingered chicken
with cinnamon prunes and almonds

A bouquet of spices including cinnamon,
ginger, and saffron make a sweet, golden
dish with Moroccan roots.

To prepare the spicy vegetables, quarter the onions
and core and quarter the bell peppers. Sprinkle with
the cumin and coriander seeds, drizzle with oil and
cook in a preheated oven at 400°F for 30 minutes, or
until tender and with crispy edges.

To prepare the chicken, rub the pieces with ground
ginger, salt, and lots of freshly ground black pepper.
Set aside for 30 minutes.

Meanwhile, place the prunes in a saucepan with cold
water to cover. Add the cinnamon stick, bring to a
boil, and simmer for 20 minutes.

Melt the butter in a casserole dish and, when
bubbling, add the almonds and stir-fry until golden.
Remove and drain on kitchen paper.

Slice the onions, add to the casserole and sauté
gently until softened and transparent.

Add the saffron and cinnamon, cook for 1 minute,
then add the chicken and sauté until golden.

Add the prunes, together with their poaching liquid,
cover, and simmer for 30 minutes, then remove
the cinnamon stick.

Sprinkle the chicken with the almonds and serve with
the spicy vegetables and steamed couscous.

8 chicken pieces

1 teaspoon
ground ginger

1⅓ cups pitted prunes

1 cinnamon stick

6 tablespoons butter

4 cups whole
blanched almonds

2 Spanish onions

½ teaspoon saffron

2–3 teaspoons
ground cinnamon

salt and pepper

steamed couscous,
to serve

spicy vegetables

4 small red onions

4 red bell peppers

1 tablespoon
cumin seeds

2 teaspoons
coriander seeds

salt and pepper

oil, for drizzling

Serves 4

Vegetables

Vegetable tagine
with sliced apricots

The tagine, named after the conical cooking pot used in North Africa, is one of the glories of Moroccan cooking, and can be made with lamb, chicken, or vegetables. Use red lentils instead of yellow split peas to produce a thick, spicy gravy to soak up the couscous.

Finely slice the bell pepper, cut the sweet potato into chunks, and blanch, peel, seed, and chop the tomatoes. Place the split peas in a saucepan, pour in the stock, add the garlic and onions, bring to a boil and simmer for 20 minutes. Stir in all the vegetables, spices, lemon juice, honey, and apricots, return to a boil and simmer for 15 to 20 minutes more. Sprinkle with the toasted cumin seeds and serve with steamed couscous.

1 green bell pepper

1 medium sweet potato

1 lb. tomatoes

½ cup yellow split peas, rinsed

1½ cups vegetable stock

1 garlic clove, crushed

8 oz. pearl onions or shallots

8 oz. baby carrots

pinch of cinnamon

pinch of ground ginger

½ teaspoon cayenne

juice of 1 lemon

1 teaspoon honey

4 dried apricots, finely sliced

to serve

½ teaspoon toasted cumin seeds

steamed couscous

Serves 4

Spicy potatoes
with garlic three-seed sauce

Potatoes form a wonderful base for spiced
sauces. This recipe, served with rice and
lentils, is great for vegetarians and it's a
treat for non-vegetarians too, when served
with plain or spicy meat dishes.

Heat half the oil in a large skillet, add the sliced
potatoes and gently sauté until cooked and golden
brown. Drain on paper towels.
Add the remaining oil to the skillet, add the onion
and gently sauté until golden. Stir in the spices, bay
leaves, chiles, and garlic. Cook for 1 minute, then
add the sugar and chopped tomatoes.
Bring the mixture to a boil, then reduce the heat and
simmer for an additional 10 minutes.
Add about 2½ cups water, return to a boil, then
simmer, stirring regularly, for 10 minutes.
Add the potatoes and mix gently until evenly coated
with the spicy sauce.
Simmer for 5 minutes to reheat, then serve.

½ cup olive oil

2 lb. potatoes, thinly
sliced, rinsed, and dried

three-seed sauce

3 large onions,
finely chopped

1 teaspoon
fenugreek seeds

1½ tablespoons
fennel seeds

1 tablespoon black
mustard seeds

1½ teaspoons turmeric

3 fresh bay leaves

4 hot chiles
finely slice

1–6 garlic clove
(depending on taste
mince

1 teaspoon suga

2 lb. ripe tomatoe
blanched, peele
seeded and choppe

Serves

Braised eggplant
with spiced yogurt

This is a modern update of the great Turkish classic dish *Imam bayaldi,* which means *the priest fainted.* No one has ever figured out why he fainted—though some say it was from the pleasure of being offered such a delicious concoction.

Cut the eggplant into ½-inch slices.
Blanch, peel, seed, and dice the tomatoes.
Heat half the oil in a skillet and cook the onion gently until softened and golden.
Add the tomatoes, garlic, cloves, cayenne, cinnamon, cumin seeds, currants, and mint, and cook over a low heat for 10 minutes.
Heat the remaining oil in another skillet until very hot, add the eggplant and cook until deep brown.
Mix the eggplant into the onion and tomato mixture.
Allow to cool, then season to taste.
To make the spiced yogurt, mix the yogurt, cumin seeds, coriander, and cilantro leaves together in a small bowl and serve with the eggplant.

another modern u|

3 medium eggplants

6 large plum tomatoes

½ cup olive oil

1 onion, finely diced

1 garlic clove, minced

1 teaspoon cloves

pinch of cayenne

2 cinnamon sticks

1 teaspoon cumin seeds

3 tablespoons currants

2 tablespoons chopped fresh mint leaves

salt and pepper

spiced yogurt

⅔ cup yogurt

1 tablespoon toasted cumin seeds

½ teaspoon ground coriander

2 tablespoons chopped fresh cilantro leaves

Serves 4

ulinary classic—

rom **Turkish** cookery

Oven-roasted peppers
filled with spiced risotto

If you're serving this dish to vegetarians, use vegetable stock instead of chicken stock. Risotto rice makes a much more creamy, delicious filling than if you used ordinary long-grain rice, and the pignoli nuts produce a delicious, buttery crunch in contrast.

Cut the bell peppers in half lengthwise, and seed. Heat the oil in a large skillet, add the onions and salt, and sauté until golden, stirring occasionally. Add the pignoli nuts and sauté until golden. Stir in the rice and cook for 3 minutes. Add a little hot stock, followed by the currants, tomato puree, sugar, allspice, chili powder, oregano, cumin, and cinnamon. Cook over a low heat until the rice is half cooked, then cool. Stir in the mint and lemon juice, tossing well.

Place the filling in the bell pepper halves, then transfer to a roasting pan and cook in a preheated oven at 350°F for 30 minutes. Serve with lemon wedges.

10 small bell peppers

3 tablespoons olive oil

2 onions, grated

1½ teaspoons salt

½ cup pignoli nuts

½ cup risotto rice

scant 2 cups
hot chicken stock

3 tablespoons
dried currants

1 tablespoon
tomato puree

1 teaspoon sugar

1 teaspoon
ground allspice

pinch of chili powder

pinch of oregano

pinch of cumin

pinch of cinnamon

2 tablespoons finely
sliced fresh mint leaves

2 tablespoons
lemon juice

8 lemon wedges,
to serve

Serves 4

Cabbage potato gratin
with ham and juniper berries

Juniper berries are a very European spice—
particularly popular because they didn't
have to be imported from the exotic orient,
but could be gathered in the hedgerows.
They are the main flavoring ingredient of gin,
and are well suited to dishes of pork, paté,
smoked meats, or game—and cabbage too.

Melt the butter in a skillet, add the onion and juniper
berries and sauté gently until softened and
transparent. Stir in the cabbage, cover with a lid, and
gently cook for about 10 minutes until just wilted.
Stir in the ham, cream, and apple juice, then spoon
into a large oval gratin pan.
Place the potato on top, with the slices overlapping,
then sprinkle with cheese and bake in a preheated
oven at 350°F until the potatoes are tender.
Serve as the main dish for a winter lunch, or for
dinner, as an accompaniment to meat dishes,
especially pork and game.

4 tablespoons butter

1 onion, sliced

1 tablespoon juniper
berries, crushed

1 head of Savoy
cabbage, shredded

4 oz. serrano ham,
shredded

1¼ cups heavy cream

1 cup apple juice

1 lb. potatoes, sliced

½ cup Gruyère
cheese, grated

Serves

that

is a perfect partn

ean spice, the **juniper berry**,

ham, game, and cabbage

Pickles

Above, from left, Pickled lemons
(recipe page 52), Candied kumquats
(page 53), and Pumpkin spice
pickle (page 52).

Pickled lemons

To use, discard the flesh and eat the peel
only—with poached meat or couscous dishes.

12 lemons

1 cup coarse sea salt,
or more if necessary

2–3 fresh bay leaves

2 cinnamon sticks

2 cloves

16 peppercorns

juice of 3–4 lemons

Cut the lemons in quarters with a sharp knife,
leaving them attached at the stem end for the last
½ inch. Place 1 to 2 tablespoons of salt in each jar.
Stuff the lemons with the remaining salt and re-form
them into their original shape. Pack them tightly into
jars, adding the bay leaves and spices as you pack.
Add any remaining salt, then pour in the lemon juice.
Seal the jars and store in the pantry for 4 to 5 weeks
before using, inverting the jar from time to time.

Makes two
1-pint jars

Pumpkin spice pickle

Pumpkin pickle is such a glorious color—the bonus is
that it also tastes fabulous, and gives a real lift to
cheese and meats.

3 pints white
wine vinegar

4 lb. fresh pumpkin

3 lb. sugar

1 tablespoon celery salt

6-inch piece of fresh
ginger, minced

2 cinnamon sticks

1 tablespoon white
mustard seed

10 cloves

Place the sugar and vinegar in a saucepan and boil
for 10 to 15 minutes. Peel, seed, and dice the
pumpkin, place in a bowl, pour in the vinegar mixture
and refrigerate overnight. Next day, drain off the
liquid into a preserving pan. Add the remaining
ingredients, bring to a boil, then add the pumpkin.
Simmer for 3 hours or until the mixture is thickened.
Pack into warm, sterilized Mason jars. Seal while still
hot. Keep for 1 month before using.

Makes four
1-pint jars

Candied kumquats

A colorful, unusual recipe to serve with ice cream and other desserts. An alternative recipe is to fill Mason jars with kumquats, add a few cloves, a cinnamon stick, and 2 tablespoons of sugar to each jar, then cover with brandy. Seal and set aside for 2 to 6 months. Use the sliced fruit with char-grilled duck breasts and the kumquat brandy to flame the meat, or serve as a liqueur with desserts or coffee.

1 lb. kumquats

2 cups sugar

1 cup cider vinegar

½ cup water

2 cinnamon sticks

10 whole cloves

2 whole star anise

Makes two 1-pint jars

Wash the kumquats well, discarding any stems. Place in a saucepan, cover with water and bring to a boil. Reduce the heat and simmer for about 5 minutes. Drain in a colander and refresh under cold water. Place all the remaining ingredients in a large saucepan and bring to a boil. Add the kumquats. Reduce the heat to low and poach gently for about 15 minutes until the fruits are very tender. Sterilize 2 Mason jars by placing in a deep saucepan, pouring over boiling water to cover, then simmering gently for 15 minutes. Using a slotted spoon, transfer the kumquats to the sterilized Mason jars. Cool the syrup to room temperature and pour over the kumquats. Seal the jars and keep in the refrigerator for up to 2 months.

Sweet things

Spicy chocolate
and fig "cupcake" desserts

A favorite recipe based on a feature in *Marie-Claire* magazine on that most sensual of ingredients—chocolate. These are rather homey desserts, but very warming, and perfect with maple syrup and vanilla custard or the gingered crème fraîche on page 59.

Cream the butter and sugar together until light and fluffy, then gradually beat in the eggs. Sift the dry ingredients together, add the dried figs, then fold into the egg mixture.

Spoon the mixture into 4 lightly buttered teacups or small ovenproof bowls. Cover each one with a piece of wax paper, place in a steamer over boiling water, cover, and steam for about 1 hour.

Serve with warm maple syrup poured over, and vanilla custard sauce, if using.

½ cup sweet butter, softened

½ cup firmly packed dark brown sugar

2 eggs

¾ cup all-purpose flour, sieved

2 tablespoon cocoa

pinch of ground cinnamon

pinch of ground ginger

pinch of ground coriander

½ cup chopped dried figs

to serve

warm maple syrup

vanilla custard sauce (optional)

Serves 4

Vanilla bean custard
with spicy cookies

An easy, pretty dessert to serve mid-week—
perfect for when friends drop by for dinner
and you want to give them something
fabulous to end the meal.

To make the cookies, sift the dry ingredients together. Gently warm the syrup until hot and runny. Stir in the butter and, when melted, scrape into a bowl. Mix in the dry ingredients to form a dough. Chill for 1 hour, then roll out to ¼ inch thick. Cut out rounds with a cookie cutter and place on a lightly greased baking sheet. Cook in a preheated oven at 375°F for 10 to 12 minutes. Remove from the oven and cool on a wire rack.

To make the custard, heat the cream and vanilla beans in a saucepan. Remove the beans, split them, scrape the seeds into the cream, then return the beans to the pan. Remove the pan from the heat and infuse for 10 minutes. Remove the beans. Beat the egg yolks and whole egg together, add the sugar, and beat until pale and creamy. Stir in the cornstarch and beat in the vanilla infused cream. Spoon the mixture into 6 small ovenproof dishes or glasses, cover with foil or wax paper and place in a roasting pan half filled with water. Cook in a preheated oven at 325°F for 45 to 60 minutes until just set and firm to the touch.

Serve with the spicy biscuits, the segmented oranges, if using, and a glass of sweet dessert wine.

1 cup cream

1–2 vanilla beans

3 egg yolks

1 whole egg

½ cup superfine sugar

1 teaspoon cornstarch

segmented oranges,
to serve (optional)

spicy cookies

1 cup self-rising flour

½ teaspoon baking soda

1 teaspoon ground
mixed spice

2 tablespoon
superfine sugar

3 oz. golden syrup

4 tablespoon
sweet butter

Serves

an easy but **spectacular** dessert—

spicy cookies with a **fragrant** vanilla custard

Orange cardamom tart
with ginger cream

A spectacular dessert—just don't tell anyone it's so easy to make. For a stronger flavor of orange and cardamom, don't strain the mixture before baking. You could also use the more traditional powdered ginger to make the cream, but fresh ginger adds a brighter flavor.

To make the pastry, mix the butter and flour until the mixture resembles fine breadcrumbs. Fold in the egg yolks and sugar, adding enough cold water to bind. Chill for 10 minutes, then roll out on a floured surface. Use to line a 9-inch false bottomed tart pan. Chill for 20 minutes, then prick the base with a fork and bake in a preheated oven at 400°F, for about 15 minutes until just golden. Place the orange juice, cardamom seeds, and grated zest in a saucepan, heat gently, then remove from the heat and leave to infuse. Mix the cornstarch with about 1 tablespoon of water, then stir into the infused orange juice, together with the eggs, egg yolk, and sugar. Pour into a non-stick saucepan and cook gently, at just below simmering point, until thickened. Remove from the heat and beat in the butter. Allow to cool slightly. Pour into the tart shell and bake in the oven at 400°F for 18 to 20 minutes until set. Leave to cool. Beat the ginger cream ingredients together and serve with the cooled tart.

½ cup cold sweet butter,
cut into small pieces

2 cups all-purpose flour

2 egg yolks

1 tablespoon sugar

**orange and
cardamom filling**

1 cup orange juice, plus
grated rind of 2 oranges

1 tablespoon
cardamom seeds

1 tablespoon cornstarch

3 eggs

1 egg yolk

½ cup sugar

½ cup sweet butter,
roughly diced

ginger cream

1 cup crème fraîche

½-inch piece of
fresh ginger, minced

Serves 4

Spicy pear pastries
sprinkled with cinnamon

These individual pastries make perfect desserts or coffee-time nibbles. You can vary the fruit according to the season—a row of pink, early forced rhubarb is pretty for springtime. Use ready rolled puff pastry if you can—it saves lots of time!

4 small pears, peeled, halved, and cored

4 star anise, crushed

4 cloves, crushed

1 vanilla bean

zest of 1 lemon, cut into fine julienne strips

2 tablespoons superfine sugar

12 oz. ready rolled puff pastry

1 egg, beaten

2 tablespoons unrefined light brown sugar

pinch of ground cinnamon

mascarpone cheese or whipped cream, to serve

Makes 8 pastries

To poach the pears, place the spices, lemon zest, and sugar in a saucepan with about ½ pint water and bring to a boil. Add the pears and simmer lightly for about 10 to 15 minutes until just tender. Leave to cool in the liquid so they absorb all the flavors of the spices.

Meanwhile, roll out the puff pastry on a floured surface to a rectangle 12 x 18 inches, then cut into eight 4-inch squares.

Place on a baking tray sprinkled with cold water. Trim a strip off each side ¼ inch wide, brush with beaten egg and place on top of each edge of the squares to form a frame. Prick the base of the pastry with a fork then chill for 30 to 60 minutes.

Lift the pears from the poaching liquid, drain well, and pat dry with paper towels.

Place one half on each pastry shell, then sprinkle with sugar and cinnamon.

Bake in a preheated oven at 400°F for about 10 to 15 minutes until the pastry is puffed up and golden. Serve warm, with mascarpone or whipped cream.

Chocolate muffins
with orange and allspice

Beautiful for breakfast, luscious for lunch,
and absolutely fabulous with tea or coffee—
these muffins are made with allspice, which
really does taste like a melange of spices.

2 cups all-purpose flour

1 tablespoon
baking powder

½ teaspoon baking soda

2 tablespoons
unsweetened cocoa

6 tablespoons
firmly packed
soft brown sugar

½ teaspoon
ground allspice

2 oz. unsweetened
dark chocolate

grated rind of 1 orange

1 egg

1 cup milk

Makes 12

Place the flour, baking powder, baking soda, cocoa,
brown sugar, and allspice in a bowl. Break the
chocolate into pieces and stir it into the bowl
together with the orange rind.
Beat the egg and milk together until well blended (do
not overmix), then fold into the dry ingredients.
Spoon the mixture into 12 paper muffin cups, then
place in a muffin tray.
Bake in a preheated oven at 400°F for 15 minutes, or
until risen and firm to the touch.

Index

Conversion Chart

Weights and measures have been
rounded up or down slightly to ma[
measuring easier.

volume equivalents:

american	metric	imp
1 teaspoon	5 ml	
1 tablespoon	15 ml	
¼ cup	60 ml	2 fl.
⅓ cup	75 ml	2½
½ cup	125 ml	4 fl.
⅔ cup	150 ml	5 fl.
		(¼
¾ cup	175 ml	6 fl.
1 cup	250 ml	8 fl.

weight equivalents: **measureme**

imperial	metric	inches	
1 oz.	25 g	¼ inch	
2 oz.	50 g	½ inch	
3 oz.	75 g	¾ inch	
4 oz.	125 g	1 inch	
5 oz.	150 g	2 inches	
6 oz.	175 g	3 inches	
7 oz.	200 g	4 inches	
8 oz.	250 g	5 inches	
9 oz.	275 g	6 inches	
10 oz.	300 g	7 inches	
11 oz.	325 g	8 inches	
12 oz.	375 g	9 inches	
13 oz.	400 g	10 inches	
14 oz.	425 g	11 inches	
15 oz.	475 g	12 inches	
16 oz.			
(1 lb.)	500 g		
2 1b.	1 kg		

oven temperatures:

225°F	110°C	Gas ¼
250°F	120°C	Gas ½
275°F	140°C	Gas 1
300°F	150°C	Gas 2
325°F	160°C	Gas 3
350°F	180°C	Gas 4
375°F	190°C	Gas 5
400°F	200°C	Gas 6
425°F	220°C	Gas 7
450°F	230°C	Gas 8
475°F	240°C	Gas 9